First World War
and Army of Occupation
War Diary
France, Belgium and Germany

40 DIVISION
120 Infantry Brigade,
Brigade Trench Mortar Battery
26 June 1916 - 31 August 1916

WO95/2612/5

The Naval & Military Press Ltd
www.nmarchive.com

Published in association with The National Archives

Published by

The Naval & Military Press Ltd

Unit 10 Ridgewood Industrial Park,

Uckfield, East Sussex,

TN22 5QE England

Tel: +44 (0) 1825 749494

www.naval-military-press.com

www.nmarchive.com

This diary has been reprinted in facsimile from the original. Any imperfections are inevitably reproduced and the quality may fall short of modern type and cartographic standards.

© **Crown Copyright**
Images reproduced by permission of The National Archives, London, England, 2015.

Contents

Document type	Place/Title	Date From	Date To
Heading	WO95/2612 (5)		
Heading	War Diary Of 120th Trench Motar Battery Volume 2 (July 1916)		
War Diary	Bruay	26/06/1916	28/06/1916
War Diary	Les Brebis	04/07/1916	11/07/1916
War Diary	Maroc	12/07/1916	16/07/1916
War Diary	Les Brebis	17/07/1916	17/07/1916
War Diary	Calonne	21/07/1916	27/07/1916
War Diary	Les Brebis	29/07/1916	29/07/1916
War Diary	War Diary 120th Trench Mortar Battery August 1916		
War Diary	Les Brebis	01/08/1916	01/08/1916
War Diary	Loos	03/08/1916	03/08/1916
War Diary	Marus	08/08/1916	08/08/1916
War Diary	Les Brebis	11/08/1916	11/08/1916
War Diary	Calonne	15/08/1916	25/08/1916
War Diary	Les Brebis.	29/08/1916	31/08/1916

W095/26125(5)

W095/26125(5)

July

40/ Vol I

Confidential
War Diary
126th French Mortar Battery

Volume 2 (July 1916)

Secret

Army Form C. 2118.

WAR DIARY
of 120ᶠ T.M.B.
INTELLIGENCE SUMMARY

(Erase heading not required.)

Instructions regarding War Diaries and Intelligence Summaries are contained in F.S. Regs., Part II. and the Staff Manual respectively. Title Pages will be prepared in manuscript.

Place	Date	Hour	Summary of Events and Information	Remarks and references to Appendices
Bruay	26/6/16 25/6/16		Half Battery of KORL→HQ Wheelers away from their battalions to other half Battery composed of ATS 4/o + 9 Siege Rs. come into Battery Billets at Côt 7 (Bruay) After instructional periods in the trenches, the Bus Section training continues in the neighbourhood of Bruay.	
Isel Brenin	4/7/16	9:45 –15:30	Marched Gun + Leo Brenin (Billy Grenay) Via Bruin, Haisin, + St Pierre. All driver equipment were carried on 8 hand wagons.	
Leo Brenin Manoc	11/7/16 12/7/16		Training continues. Reconnaissances in Manor Reserve Section. Advance party [2 Officers + 4 NCOs] go up to 121 TMB - Manor Section. Right Half Battery take over Manor Section from 121 TMB. Then mostly spent in reporting activity, shells + enemy ammunition stores.	
Manoc Leo Brenin	13/7/16 17/7/16		4 men [Cath, Symmour] ordering sanitation man) attached to Battery of dust. Left Half Battery relieves Right Half Battery in Manoc. 121 TMB "120 TMB. 120 TMB trained in Leo Brenin meantime.	
Colonne	21/7/16		120 TMB relieves 119 TMB in Colonne (which now includes R. subsector of the old Manoc). 6 gun teams [90 guns] in line. 2 gun teams (+ 15cm) at LeBouin. Retaliation for an attack for which	
Colonne Colonne	23/7/16 27/7/16		Unsuccessful attempt to cut enemy wire at M15 a 50.93. Enemy wire + front line trench shelled + kept at M15 a 50.93. + M20 + 20.75. There was no retaliation.	
In Relief	29/7/16		Battery relieved by 119 T.M.B. + rests in Leo Brenin	

Start

Vol 24

WAR DIARY

120th Trench Mortar
Battery

Augr 1916

Army Form C. 2118

WAR DIARY
of 120 T.M.B. for August 1916.
INTELLIGENCE SUMMARY

(Erase heading not required.)

Instructions regarding War Diaries and Intelligence Summaries are contained in F. S. Regs., Part II. and the Staff Manual respectively. Title Pages will be prepared in manuscript.

Place	Date	Hour	Summary of Events and Information	Remarks and references to Appendices
Les Brebis	1/8/16		Battery in divisional Reserve in LES BREBIS.	
LOOS	3/8/16		" took over LOOS sector and North half of MAROC Sector from 121 T.M.B.	
MAROC	8/8/16		Handed over LOOS sector to 47 T.M.B. & took over South Half MAROC from 119 T.M.B.	
LES BREBIS	11/8/16		MAROC " 121 T.M.B. and went into Divisional Reserve at LES BREBIS	
CALONNE	15/8/16		Took over CALONNE sector from 119 T.M.B.	
"	18/8/16		Cooperated with other T.M's in bombardment of CITÉ Cornailles. (Successful. 1 (HE) man killed)	
"	22/8/16		" " " " Hu. = rais.	
"	23/8/16		" " " " Arsh. " "	
"	25/8/16		" " other T.M's in bombardment of CITÉ Cornailles. (Successful)	
LES BREBIS	29/8/16		Handed over CALONNE Sector to 150 T.M.B.	
"	31/8/16		Position; Divisional reserve at LES BREBIS. Billets change from Battalion Area to Specialist Area. One officer (2/L Daintree) leaves for Ludango course = Stokes Gun at CAMIQUES.	

J. Rankin Capt
OC 120 T.M.B.